W9-BGG-474

Purple As a Plum
Morado como una ciruela

written by **Molly Dingles**

illustrated by **Walter Velez**

dingles & company New Jersey

First printing

PUBLISHED BY dingles&company
P.O. Box 508 • Sea Girt, New Jersey • 08750
WEBSITE: www.dingles.com • E-MAIL: info@dingles.com

LIBRARY BINDING EDITION DISTRIBUTED BY **GUMDROP BOOKS**
P.O. Box 505 • Bethany, Missouri • 64424
(660) 425-7777

Library of Congress Catalog Card No.: 2003115149
ISBN: 1-891997-32-7

Printed in the United States of America

●

ART DIRECTED & DESIGNED BY Barbie Lambert

ENGLISH EDITED BY Andrea Curley

SPANISH EDITED BY John Page

EDUCATION CONSULTANT Kathleen P. Miller

For Joe Raymond

Molly Dingles

is the author of *Jinka Jinka Jelly Bean* and *Little Lee Lee's Birthday Bang*. As Judy Zocchi, she has written the *Paulie & Sasha* series. She is a writer and lyricist who holds a bachelor's degree in fine arts/theater from Mount Saint Mary's College and a master's degree in educational theater from New York University. She lives in Manasquan, New Jersey, with her husband, David.

Walter Velez

was born in New York. He attended the High School of Art and Design and later the School of Visual Arts. He has done illustration work for many major book and gaming companies. He is known for the popular series *Thieves World* as well as the *Myth* series for Ace Books. He has also produced trading cards for *Goosebumps* and *Dune*. In addition, Walter has illustrated several *Star Wars* books for Random House. He lives in Queens, New York, with his wife, Kriti, and daughter, Kassandra.

The Community of Color series is more than just a series of books about colors. The series demonstrates how individual people, places, and things combine to form a community. It allows children to view the world in segments and then experience the wonderment and value of the community as a whole.

Purple as an eggplant

Morado
como una berenjena

Purple tulips
in a bunch

Tulipanes morados
en un ramo

Purple as a plum

Morado
como una ciruela

Purple juice
to drink at lunch

Jugo morado para
beber en el almuerzo

Purple as a violet

**Morado
como una violeta**

Purple ice pops
for a snack

Paletas
de helado moradas
para una merienda

Purple as some jam

Morado
como mermelada

Purple gumdrops
in a pack

Pastillas
de goma moradas
en una cajetilla

Purple as a lilac

Morado como una lila

Purple awning on a shop

Toldo morado en una tienda

Purple as a grape

●

Morado como una uva

Purple bubble gum to pop

Chicle globo morado para estallar

The color Purple is all around.

El color morado está en todas partes.

ABOUT COLOR

Use the Community of Color series to teach your child to identify the most basic colors and to help him or her relate these colors to objects in the real world. ASK:

- What color is this book about?
- Can you name the purple things in this market?
- Can you find a purple vegetable in this picture?
- What purple fruits are in this picture?

ABOUT COMMUNITY

Use the Community of Color series to teach your child how he or she is an important part of the community. Explain to your child what a community is.

- A community is a place where people live, work, and play together.
- Your family is a community.
- Your school is a community.
- Your neighborhood is a community.
- The world is one big community.

Everyone plays an important part in making a community work - moms, dads, boys, girls, police officers, firefighters, teachers, mail carriers, garbage collectors, store clerks, and even animals are all important parts of a community. USE THESE QUESTIONS TO FURTHER THE CONVERSATION:

- How are the people in this market interacting with one another?
- How are the people different from one another? How are they the same?
- What do they have in common?
- How is the community you see in this book like your community? How is it different?
- Describe your community.

ABOUT FEELINGS

Colors can describe as well as evoke different emotions. Encourage your child to describe the feelings that the color purple inspires.

- How does the color purple make you feel?
- Name your favorite purple thing in this book. Why is it your favorite?
- Name your favorite purple thing at home. Why is it your favorite?
- Can you tell how the people in the picture feel by looking at their faces? Do you ever feel the same way? When? Why?

TRY SOMETHING NEW... Help those in need! The next time you go to a market buy a jar of grape jam and donate it to your local food bank.

community of color series